FASCIN
FAC
ABOU
BIBLE

C000151809

FASCINATING FACTS ABOUT THE BIBLE

Compiled by Phyllis Bailey

Insofar as is practical the editors have verified
the information here provided.

REVIEW AND HERALD® PUBLISHING ASSOCIATION
Hagerstown, MD 21740

Copyright © 1976 by the
Review and Herald® Publishing Association
Library of Congress Card No. 74-28754
Revised 1991

Printed in U.S.A.

ISBN 0-8280-0642-3

CONTENTS

THE BIBLE

This book contains the mind of God, the state of man, the way of salvation, the doom of sinners, and the happiness of believers. Its doctrines are holy, its precepts are binding, its histories are true, and its decisions are immutable. Read it to be wise, believe in it to be safe, and practice it to be holy. It contains light to direct you, food to support you, and comfort to cheer you. It is the traveler's map, the pilgrim's staff, the pilot's compass, the soldier's sword, and the Christian's charter. Here paradise is restored, heaven opened, and the gates of hell disclosed. Christ is its grand object; our good, its design; and the glory of God, its end. It should fill the memory, rule the heart, and guide the feet. Read it slowly, frequently, and prayerfully. It is a mine of wealth, a paradise of glory, and a river of pleasure. It is given you in life, will be opened in the judgment, and be remembered forever. It involves the highest responsibility, will reward the greatest labor, and will condemn all who trifle with its sacred contents.

Author Unknown

THE BOOKS OF THE BIBLE

In Genesis the world was made by God's creative hand;
    In Exodus the Hebrews marched to gain the Promised Land;
Leviticus contains the law, holy, and just and good.
    Numbers records the tribes enrolled—all sons of Abraham's blood.
Moses, in Deuteronomy records God's mighty deeds;
    Brave Joshua into Canaan's land the host of Israel leads.
In Judges their rebellion oft provokes the Lord to smite,
    But Ruth records the faith of one well pleasing in His sight.
In First and Second Samuel of Jesse's son we read.
    Ten Tribes in First and Second Kings revolted from his seed.
The First and Second Chronicles see Judah captive made;
    But Ezra leads a remnant back by princely Cyrus' aid.
The city wall of Zion Nehemiah builds again,
    While Esther saves her people from the plots of wicked men.
In Job we read how faith will live beneath affliction's rod,
    And David's psalms are precious songs to every child of God.
The Proverbs like a goodly string of choicest pearls appear.
    Ecclesiastes teaches man how vain are all things here.
The mystic Song of Solomon exalts sweet Sharon's Rose;
    Whilst Christ, the Saviour and the King, the rapt Isaiah shows.
The warning Jeremiah apostate Israel scorns;
    His plaintive Lamentations their awful downfall mourns.
Ezekiel tells in wondrous words of dazzling mysteries;
    While kings and empires yet to come, Daniel in vision sees.
Of judgment and of mercy, Hosea loves to tell;
    Joel describes the blessed days when God with man shall dwell.
Among Tekoa's herdsmen Amos received his call;
    While Obadiah prophesies of Edom's final fall.
Jonah enshrines a wondrous type of Christ, our risen Lord,
    Micah pronounces Judah lost—lost, but again restored.
Nahum declares on Nineveh just judgment shall be poured,
    A view of Chaldea's coming doom Habakkuk's visions give;
Next, Zephaniah warns the Jews to turn, repent, and live.
    Haggai wrote to those who saw the Temple built again,
And Zechariah prophesied of Christ's triumphant reign.
    Malachi was the last who touched the high prophetic chord;
Its final notes sublimely show the coming of the Lord.
Matthew and Mark and Luke and John the holy Gospels wrote,

Describing how the Saviour died—His life, and all He taught.
Acts proves how God the apostles owned with signs in every place.
Saint Paul, in Romans, teaches us how man is saved by grace.
The apostle, in Corinthians, instructs, exhorts, reproves.
Galatians shows that faith in Christ alone the Father loves.
Ephesians and Philippians tell what Christians ought to be;
Colossians bids us live to God and for eternity.
In Thessalonians we are taught the Lord will come from heaven.
In Timothy and Titus a bishop's rule is given.
Philemon marks a Christian's love, which only Christians know.
Hebrews reveals the gospel prefigured by the law.
James teaches, Without holiness faith is but vain and dead.
Saint Peter points the narrow way in which the saints are led.
John in his three Epistles on love delights to dwell.
Saint Jude gives awful warning of judgment, wrath and hell.
The Revelation prophesies of that tremendous day,
When Christ—and Christ alone—shall be the trembling sinner's
stay.

Author Unknown

BIBLE BOOKS IN A NUTSHELL

The term *Bible* (Greek, *biblia*) means "little books."

OLD TESTAMENT

GENESIS: "Birth" or "origins"   Author: Moses
    Tells the history of Creation and carries on to the death of Joseph, a period of more than 2,000 years.

EXODUS: "The way out" or "going out" Author: Moses
    Relates the history of Israel's departure from Egypt, and the giving of the law and building of the tabernacle.

LEVITICUS: "Law of the priests"   Author: Moses
    Describes the ceremonial laws and tells the way the people were to worship God. It was after referred to as the "handbook of the priests."

NUMBERS   Author: Moses
    Gives the census of the people. It is a sequel to the book of Exodus. Relates the Israelite story from Sinai until the arrival at the borders of Moab.

DEUTERONOMY: "Second legislation"   Author: Moses
    Repeats the law and traces God's workings for Israel to the border of Canaan.
    Records the counsels and songs given by Moses just before the nation's passage of the Jordan, and his death.

JOSHUA   Author: Probably Joshua
    Named after Joshua, the successor of Moses. The book is a continuation of the history of Israel. Describes their entering the Promised Land and gives the division of the land and of settlement.

JUDGES   Author: Unknown
    Covers the history of Israel during their first 350 years in the Land of Promise.

RUTH   Author: Unknown
    The events recorded in this book happened early in the period of

the Judges, but are told in a style that contrasts greatly with that of the book of Judges. Records the early lineage of the royal family of Judah, from which Christ sprang 1,000 years later.

1 SAMUEL   Author: Composite authorship

A record of a period of about 100 years, from about 1100 to 1011 B.C. It covers the time of Samuel, the kingship of Saul, and the experiences of David before Saul's death.

2 SAMUEL   Author or compiler: Unknown

A description of the reign of David. 1 and 2 Samuel were originally one book.

1 AND 2 KINGS   Author: Compilation

In the Hebrew Bible 1 and 2 Kings were originally one book. They record events of the reign of Solomon and the other kings of Judah and of Israel, covering a period of about 400 years.

In addition to the record of these kings, we find in the books accounts of the ministry of Elijah, the most outstanding of the ancient prophets, and of Elisha.

1 AND 2 CHRONICLES   Author: Probably Ezra

These books were composed or at least completed in the late fifth century B.C., and are thought to be perhaps the last of the Old Testament Biblical books written.

EZRA, NEHEMIAH   Author: Ezra

In the Hebrew Bible, until A.D. 1448, these two books appeared as one. The time covered by these two books is about 200 years, although there are large time gaps in the records. Their history covers the restoration of the Jews from their captivity, and rebuilding of the Temple and city. They show how the prophecies of Isaiah and Jeremiah were fulfilled.

ESTHER   Author: Unknown

The story of the young Jewess who became queen of Persia and saved her people from destruction.

This book is the only one in the Bible not containing the word *God,* yet God's providential care for the people is seen throughout the book.

In the Bible this book follows Nehemiah, but in history the events in Esther occurred some 30 years before the story of Nehemiah.

JOB   Author: Probably Moses
The story of a godly man, tried terribly by sudden, unaccountable reverses, misunderstood and misrepresented by his friends, plunged into the depths of discouragement, yet holding on to God and finding, at last, an unshakable faith in Him. The story closes with Job being blessed in "the latter end" more than at the beginning.

PSALMS: "Songs"   Author: David and others
This book contains 150 songs of praise, prayers, and petitions, intended for use in the worship of God. Many were written by David. Psalm 90 is a prayer of Moses. Two psalms are by Solomon.

The book of Psalms contains both the longest and shortest chapters in the entire Bible.

In this book can be found words for the sick and suffering, the poor and needy, the prisoner and exile, the man in danger or persecuted, or the sinner. Almost every aspect of man's relationship to God is touched upon here.

PROVERBS: "Proverbial sayings"   Author: Solomon and others
In Proverbs we read the wise sayings of Solomon, who was one of the greatest kings of ancient times. In these proverbs practically every relationship in life is mentioned. Solomon wrote 3,000 proverbs and 1,005 songs (1 Kings 3:31, 32).

ECCLESIASTES: "Preacher"   Author: Solomon
This book of poetry has been so named because it contains the meditations and sermons of the wise man, Solomon, in which he points out the vanity of earthly things. He uses the phrase "under the sun" 28 times.

This book holds up a danger sign against sin, and closes with a call to the young that they might be spared some of life's bitter experiences.

SONG OF SOLOMON   Author: Solomon
The Song of Solomon is a poem with love as its theme. It may be used to illustrate the love between Christ and His church.

ISAIAH   Author: Isaiah
This book is filled with messages and prophecies of the coming of Christ, or the Messiah, and His kingdom. In these messages of encouragement are some of the most graphic portrayals of the Messiah found in the Old Testament. Also the coming destruction

of Jerusalem. Isaiah spent his life trying to get Judah to become acquainted with God.

JEREMIAH: "Yahweh establishes"   Author: Jeremiah
   Though not arranged chronologically, the book of Jeremiah gives prophecies concerning the captivity of Judah, its sufferings, and its final restoration. Seeing the coming Babylonian captivity, Jeremiah rebukes, warns, threatens, and denounces the sins of the people, beseeching them to return to God's commandments.
   The message of this book shows the certainty of God's judgment against sin, but points to His tenderness and boundless love. No other prophet had as difficult a task as Jeremiah. He had to stand alone for God in the midst of the apostasy of his own people.

LAMENTATIONS   Author: Jeremiah
   Composed of five poems, corresponding to its five chapters, Lamentations gives to its author, Jeremiah, the title "The Weeping Prophet." The occasion for this book was the destruction of Jerusalem by Babylon, and the captivity of its inhabitants.

EZEKIEL: "When God will strengthen"   Author: Ezekiel
   The first main section of this book (chapters 1-24), which describes the apostasy for which Israel would be punished, was written before the fall of Jerusalem, and the next section (chapters 25-32), afterward. The remainder points in hope to the restoration.
   "The word of the Lord came unto me" appears some 49 times in this book. It is recorded that God called Ezekiel "son of man" 100 times.

DANIEL: "God is my judge"   Author: Daniel
   Contains a predictive prophetic sweep of history from the prophet's day to the end of time. The basic prophetic book of the Bible.

HOSEA: "Jehovah has saved"   Author: Hosea
   Using as an illustration his own unhappy experience with his wife, Hosea deals with God's great love for His wayward people, Israel. In spite of the dark picture painted of the sins of his nation, Hosea holds out hope for them if they will repent.

JOEL: "Jehovah is God"   Author: Joel
   A call to ancient Israel for reformation, an explanation of why it is necessary, and a message that through repentance will be

found blessings from God, material and spiritual.

AMOS: "A burden bearer"　　　　　　　Author: Amos
Amos' chief purpose was to call the attention of God's people, living in a time of prosperity and luxury, to a recognition of their sins and bring them to repentance. He rebukes every evil practice, counting it a duty to warn all of the divine judgments to come on all who persist in doing iniquity.

OBADIAH: "Servant of Jehovah"　　　　　Author: Obadiah
This is the shortest book in the Old Testament, containing only 21 verses. Obadiah prophesies the destruction of Edom (or descendants of Esau), because of their hostility toward the Jews.

JONAH: "Dove"　　　　　　　　　　Author: Jonah
Jonah is the only book of the prophets that is written in narrative form. It is the story of an obstinate prophet who said No to God when asked to go to Nineveh, one of the greatest cities in the world, to warn it of its destruction because of its sins.

After his experience of being swallowed by a fish he was given a second chance, and later carried out the commission. Because of the universality of God's love shown in the book, it has been called a counterpart of John 3:16.

MICAH: "Who is like Jehovah?"　　　　　Author: Micah
Micah and Isaiah were contemporaries, and their prophecies are much alike.

Micah's burden was the sins of the people, especially Judah's, knowing they would lead to the Babylonian captivity. The book closes with a prophecy of the glory of the Messianic kingdom.

NAHUM: "Comforted"　　　　　　　　Author: Nahum
Nahum's prophecy of the downfall of Assyria was written about 150 years after Jonah's warning the Ninevites and their subsequent repentance, which did not last. The siege and fall of Nineveh is described. The Medes and Babylonians completely destroyed the city in 612 B.C.

HABAKKUK: From the Hebrew verb *to embrace* Author: Habakkuk
This short book deals mainly with the question Why does God permit sinners to flourish while He seems indifferent to their wicked acts? God answers the prophet's rash questions by assuring

14

him that when the time is ripe He will act.

God's word to Habakkuk in chapter 2:4—"The just shall live by his faith"—is quoted 3 times in the New Testament (Romans 1:17; Galatians 3:11; Hebrews 10:38).

ZEPHANIAH: "Jehovah has hidden"   Author: Zephaniah

Zephaniah seems to have been a descendant of King Hezekiah of Judah (Zephaniah 1:1). His book is about the judgments that would fall upon Judah and surrounding nations for their sins. The term "day of the Lord," which is used several times, refers more to God's judgments that were to come upon those nations than to the final day of judgment.

HAGGAI: "Festal"   Author: Haggai

This prophet was the first of 3 to prophesy after the exile. His message was to persuade the people to rebuild the Temple, and to bring comfort and encouragement to a discouraged nation. He says, "The glory of this latter house shall be greater than of the former, saith the Lord of hosts: and in this place will I give peace, saith the Lord of hosts" (Haggai 2:9).

ZECHARIAH: "Jehovah remembers"   Author: Zechariah

Zechariah, like Haggai, was used by God to stir the remnant Jews who returned to Babylon after the 70 years of captivity to rebuild the Temple.

Zechariah also foretells the coming of the Saviour and His work, more than any other prophet other than Isaiah. He predicted His entry into Jerusalem on a colt (Zechariah 9:9); His betrayal for 30 pieces of silver (chapter 11:12, 13); His hands being pierced (chapter 12:10); His second coming on the Mount of Olives (chapter 14:3-8).

MALACHI: "My messenger"   Author: Malachi

Written about 400 years before Christ, the book of Malachi describes the terrible, progressive spiritual declension of the Jews. The degree of their apostasy is illustrated by their denial of wrong, and by their suggestion that God is unjust. For the faithful ones the prophet ends with the assurance that God will keep them in the day of judgment.

NEW TESTAMENT

MATTHEW
Author: Matthew

Matthew was a disciple of Jesus and a former publican (tax collector). Mark and Luke refer to him as Levi.

Matthew's object seems to be to show that Jesus was the long-expected Messiah, that His life was the fulfilling of the Old Testament prophecies relating to the Messiah. Thus it is that, more than a dozen times after describing some event in Jesus' life, he makes a statement such as, "that it might be fulfilled which was spoken by the prophets." By one count Matthew refers to the kingdom 55 different times, and the "kingdom of heaven" 35 times. It is said that Matthew quotes more from the Old Testament than any other New Testament writer.

Of the 15 parables recorded by Matthew all but three begin: "The kingdom of heaven is like . . ."

Matthew and Luke are the only two who wrote of the genealogy of Christ, but with noticeable differences. In Matthew His genealogy is traced back to Abraham, father of the Jewish nation (Matthew 1:1-17); Luke traces it back to Adam (Luke 3:38), the father of the human family, showing that He belongs to each one of us, as well as to the Jewish nation.

Only Matthew records the visit of the Wise Men from the East at Jesus' birth and of the flight into Egypt.

MARK
Author: Mark

Mark is described as the son of a woman named Mary (Mark 12:12), and a cousin of Paul's missionary companion Barnabas (Col. 4:10). Mark begins his Gospel by introducing John the Baptist as the herald of the Messiah. He demonstrates that Jesus is the Son of God by the works He accomplished during His brief stay on earth.

In the King James Version all but four of the sixteen chapters of Mark begin with the word *and* illustrating how Christ's life and service are a complete, perfect whole. The word *and* is said to appear 1,375 times in this short book.

Mark is the shortest of all the Gospels, and very little is found here that is not in the other Gospels. It is the first of the four Gospels to be written.

Mark, who depicts Jesus as a man of action, records twenty of Jesus' miracles in detail, but only four parables.

16

LUKE   Author: Luke

Luke was a Gentile physician, and sometime companion of
Paul (Acts 16:10-24; 2 Tim. 4:11; Col. 4:14). It is obvious from his
writings that he was an educated man, with a wide cultural back-
ground. Scholars believe he wrote for Greek readers. Thus, writing
for Gentiles, he traces Christ's ancestry back to Adam, the father of
the race. Matthew, writing for Jews, traces it back to Abraham.

Luke, the longest of the Gospels, gives the longest account of
Jesus and the only one of His childhood, including His visit to the
Temple at the age of 12. Only he records the visit of the shepherds
at His birth.

Luke's portrayal of Jesus as one with humanity, sympathetic
to human needs, is in keeping with Paul's description of him as "the
beloved physician" (Col. 4:14). Thus he relates the stories of the
good Samaritan (Luke 10:33); the publican (chapter 18:13); the
prodigal (chapter 15:11-24); Zacchaeus (chapter 19:2); and the
thief on the cross (chapter 23:43).

He alone tells of Jesus' beholding the city of Jerusalem and
weeping over it, of His bloody sweat in Gethsemane, and of His
showing mercy to the dying thief on the cross.

JOHN   Author: John

John, a Galilean from Bethsaida, on the Sea of Galilee, was
the youngest of Jesus' disciples. His Gospel, written when he was
very old, toward the close of the first century, is quite different
from the others. One reason for this is that he describes Jesus' Judean
ministry, whereas the other writers deal with His Galilean.

John begins his book by turning our minds to "the beginning"
of Creation, and portrays Jesus as God, before all things, the Creator
of all, who "was made flesh, and dwelt among us."

The key word is *believe*, which appears in the book almost 100
times. The key text is chapter 20:31. The purpose of the book is to
lead men to believe that Jesus is the Messiah, the Son of God.

John alone relates the story of Christ's first miracle at Cana,
the interview with Nicodemus, the raising of Lazarus, His commend-
ing His mother to the care of John at the cross, and the triumphant
shout, "It is finished."

ACTS   Author: Luke

The book covers approximately the years A.D. 31-63. It begins
with the ascension of Jesus and then relates something of the

17

2

growth of Christianity in Palestine and nearby countries. An important element of Acts is that it describes how the gospel broke through the exclusiveness of Judaism and spread to the Gentile world.

More than thirty times the word *witness* is used. The name of the Holy Spirit is used seventy times, and although the book is called the Acts of the Apostles, we rather see for the most part the Holy Spirit working through Peter and Paul and their companions.

ROMANS   Author: Paul

This letter of Paul is the longest and probably the most influential of all his writings. It was penned at Corinth, possibly during the winter of A.D. 57-58.

All men are sinners, in a hopeless situation, unable to do righteously, but that the grace of God provides for the pardon and perfecting of all is the apostle's theme. This is made possible through faith in Jesus Christ.

The first part of the book tells what God did for us, and the last part, what we should do for God and our fellow men.

1 CORINTHIANS   Author: Paul

Paul wrote this letter to the church of Corinth in the spring of 57 from Ephesus, where he spent 3 years. At this time Corinth was perhaps the most important city in all of Greece, noted for its wealth, trade, luxury, and licentiousness. Its principal deity was Aphrodite, the goddess of sensual love.

First Corinthians has two themes: rebuke for contentiousness and immorality, and the clarification of questions asked by the Corinthian believers.

After rebuking the Christian believers for a party spirit and immorality, Paul goes on to discuss such questions as food sacrificed to idols, the deportment of women in church, the celebration of the Lord's Supper, tongues, and the resurrection.

2 CORINTHIANS   Author: Paul

Because Paul's first letter to the Corinthian believers was well received by the majority of them, he wrote the second letter.

The theme of the first seven chapters is mainly thankfulness for the reception of his previous letter, coupled with a defense of his apostleship.

In chapters 8 and 9 he urges the Corinthian Christians to fulfill their obligations by helping the poor Christians at Jerusalem, an obligation they had neglected. In the final chapters he writes to the minority who had not accepted his rebuke in his first letter, and appeals to them to repent.

GALATIANS   Author: Paul
The date of the writing of this Epistle is uncertain: It has been dated as early as A.D. 45; it may have been written during the same winter Paul wrote Romans (A.D. 57-58).

The Epistle's theme is very similar to Romans: righteousness by faith in Jesus Christ. The treatment of the subject centers on the insistence of certain Judaizers that the keeping of prescribed requirements of Judaism—"works"—is necessary for salvation.

Paul firmly repudiates this teaching by insisting that works do not justify a man—only faith in Christ. In fact, trusting in "works of the law" makes the operation of grace impossible.

EPHESIANS   Author: Paul
This letter, written about A.D. 62, is one of the 4 the apostle Paul wrote in prison. Philippians, Colossians, and Philemon are the others.

In this Epistle Paul writes of the church as the body of Christ; and he calls for Christian unity: for the individual believer to be united to Christ, and for the Jew and Gentile to be one in Christ. And he describes the gifts of the Spirit as intended to bring unity. The last part of the Epistle is an exhortation for reformation of life, and a discussion of home relationships.

PHILIPPIANS   Author: Paul
This letter was written by Paul, during his first imprisonment, to the first church founded in Europe. A vision in which he was invited to "come over into Macedonia, and help us," brought Paul to Philippi.

This letter gives us information about Paul's situation during his Roman imprisonment, as well as of his relationship to the Philippian church. The words *joy in Christ* may well describe the theme of the book; the words *joy* or *rejoice* are used many times.

In this letter Paul expresses his gratitude for the love of the Philippians and their gifts to him.

COLOSSIANS   Author: Paul
This Epistle was also written during Paul's imprisonment in Rome. The Colossian church is infected with the false teachings of

Judaistic legalism, as was the Galatian. In addition, pagan elements, such as angel intermediaries, angel worship and "will worship," are being taught by some. Paul presents Christ as the true Mediator who only is the "hope of glory."

Though these letters are similar in style, the emphasis in each is very different.

1 THESSALONIANS   Author: Paul
During his second missionary journey Paul, accompanied by Timothy and Silas, preached three Sabbath days at Thessalonica, and during that time he founded this church. Then he went on to Berea, Athens, and Corinth. Timothy followed him later, and it was as a result of Timothy's report that the letter was written.

In the letter Paul commends the Thessalonians for their faith, love, and hope, and goes on to correct misunderstandings that had arisen regarding the resurrection and the manner of Christ's second coming. He also deals with future rewards and punishment and the doctrine of redemption.

2 THESSALONIANS   Author: Paul
It is probable that 2 Thessalonians was written only a few months after 1 Thessalonians. It seeks to correct further misunderstandings that had arisen, apparently as a result of his first Epistle. Certain emphasis by Paul seems to have given some the impression the Second Coming was imminent. Therefore the apostle prophesies of events to take place before Christ's return.

1 TIMOTHY   Author: Paul
First and second Timothy, with Titus, are called the Pastoral Epistles because they deal with the duty of ministers to their churches. Timothy, a young Greek-Jewish convert of Paul's, had accompanied the apostle on some of his travels. At the time the Epistles were written he was pastor of the important Ephesus church. This Epistle, with 2 Timothy, may be regarded as a handbook for Christian pastors and ministers. In this Epistle Paul unfolds plans for church organization and development, and emphasizes the need for sound doctrine.

2 TIMOTHY   Author: Paul
This, so far as we know, is Paul's last letter before his execution. It was penned in a Roman prison to his "dearly beloved son," Timothy, following his final arrest, apparently somewhere in Greece.

In the Epistle Paul writes of his work's being "finished" and of his expectation of death. But, forgetting himself, he seeks to strengthen Timothy and to give him final counsel regarding his ministry. He also warns him of perilous days ahead, and exhorts him to follow the example Paul himself had set.

TITUS   Author: Paul
Written to Titus, a Gentile convert of Paul's, while Titus was organizing the Christian church on the island of Crete. Earlier Paul had given Titus the difficult task of settling the differences at Corinth, and in the second letter to the Corinthians we learn how successful he was in this mission. Seventeen years after Paul's conversion Titus accompanied him and Barnabas to Jerusalem.

As in the letters to Timothy, this letter discusses in a practical way the everyday problems confronted by a young minister. It is thought to have been written between the two letters to Timothy. Paul tells Titus the qualifications of church officers (Titus 1:6-9), talks to him of the aged (chapter 2:2, 3), the youth (verses 4-6), the slaves (verses 9, 10), and how to live a Christian life.

PHILEMON   Author: Paul
This, the shortest of all Paul's letters, is addressed to Philemon, a Christian living in Colossae. It was written on behalf of Onesimus, Philemon's slave, who had run away, and had met Paul. Converted and repentant, he returns to his master with this letter from Paul. In the letter Paul entreats Philemon to receive Onesimus back as a brother in Christ. He makes himself responsible for the debts that he might owe, asking that they be charged to his (Paul's) account.

HEBREWS   Author: Paul
This book has been called the fifth Gospel. Matthew, Mark, Luke, and John describe Christ's ministry on earth; Hebrews describes His ministry in heaven.

The theme of the book is Christ's perfect sacrifice for the sins of the world—His ministry as high priest, representing us to His Father. Its message is structured around a comparison and contrast with the Old Testament symbols and their fulfillment in Christ.

This book shows that we must have the Old Testament to understand the New, and the New Testament to understand the Old.

JAMES   Author: James
The author of this letter introduces himself as "James, a servant

of God and of the Lord Jesus Christ." There are three men in the New Testament who bore this name, one of whom was the brother of our Lord. But it is not possible to discover with certainty which of the three wrote this Epistle.

This book, addressed "to the twelve tribes . . . scattered abroad," is the most Jewish in style and form of any of the New Testament books. It is sometimes referred to as the Proverbs of the New Testament because of its practical guide to Christian living and conduct.

It points out that works, and not words, are the mark of a disciple. While Paul deals with the source of our faith, James speaks of the fruits of it. Throughout the letter a contrast is made between the manifestations of true and false religion.

1 PETER
Author: Peter

This Epistle was written by Peter toward the end of his life, probably in the middle sixties A.D.

The contents of the book reflect a time of trial and suffering, and it was probably written during the widespread persecution of the Christians by the Roman authorities under the cruel Emperor Nero.

Peter admonishes the readers of this book to a life of purity and godly living, exhorting them to be faithful and steadfast. He seeks to encourage his readers in the face of persecution. Consequently he uses the terms *joy* and *glory* more than a score of times, and refers to hope several times.

Peter knew from experience what trials and suffering meant, but he gives a formula for happiness in a world that is wretched and evil. In the fifth chapter he tells his readers to cast all their cares upon God, for He cares for them.

2 PETER
Author: Peter

As in his First Epistle, Peter admonishes his readers to remain steadfast amid persecution and reminds them that the Lord will keep His promises. He warns of the dangers within the church, especially of false teachers and false prophets, and speaks of the "day of the Lord" and of the necessity of keeping oneself "without spot, and blameless."

1 JOHN
Author: John

The three Epistles of John were written by the apostle John, the writer of the fourth Gospel. They are thought to be dated A.D. 90-95, when John was quite old.

The theme of the Epistle, characteristic of John, is love. The concept is used in some way in the letter more than two dozen times.

In the letter John seeks to combat heresies that were troubling the church, especially Gnosticism. The adherents of this heresy claimed to have special knowledge. John writes of the true knowledge.

2 JOHN   Author: John

This is a personal letter addressed to an "elect lady and her children." It is the only one in the Bible addressed specifically to a woman.

The word *truth* is found 5 times in the 13 verses of this book, and *love*, 4 times. John points out that the test of our love is whether we keep God's commandments.

3 JOHN   Author: John

Written to counter schismatic tendencies on the part of one Diotrephes, this letter was sent by John to an elder named Gaius. While he writes with firmness, nevertheless the affectionate spirit of the beloved apostle shows through.

JUDE   Author: Jude

This short letter was written by Jude, believed to be a brother of Jesus. He warns against the dangers of apostasy and urges his readers to defend the faith courageously. His letter is very similar to 2 Peter.

REVELATION   Author: John

This last book of the Bible was penned by John, the author of the fourth Gospel and the 3 Epistles of John.

Revelation is the only book in the New Testament that is essentially all prophecy. Its theme is the unfolding of the future events related to the church and the world, ending in the triumph of our Lord. These revelations are given to John through Jesus, who received them from the Father (chapter 1:1).

By one estimate, there are 300 symbols used in Revelation, each with a definite meaning. Jesus is referred to as a lamb, referring to His sacrifice for His people, more than 25 times.

ABOUT THE WRITING OF THE BIBLE

As many as 40 authors wrote the Bible over a period of more than 1,500 years (from 1500 B.C. to about A.D. 100).

The 40 authors differed widely in their culture and education, and with personality and intellectual perception, and yet the books they wrote do not contradict one another.

The first books of the Bible were written by Moses, and the last by John. Moses wrote the first 5 about 3,500 years ago, and John the last, 1,600 years later.

Some 30 authors wrote the books of the Old Testament. Their lives covered a period of about 1,200 years.

The New Testament was written by 8 men in a period of about 50 years: Matthew, Mark, Luke, John, Paul, Peter, James, and Jude. At least 4 of these men were disciples of Christ.

The Bible deals with the subjects of history, biography, poetry, speeches, proverbs, songs, parables, prophecies, romances, drama, tragedies, sermons, dialog, and ethical teachings.

The English Old Testament in the Greek, or Septuagint, version is divided into 4 parts: The Pentateuch, History, Poetry, and Prophecy. The Hebrew is traditionally divided into 3 parts: The Law, the Prophets, and the Psalms. Jesus so referred to it in Luke 24:44.

The New Testament has 3 main parts: history (the 4 Gospels and Acts), doctrine (in the Epistles), and prophecy (Revelation).

The New Testament may also be grouped into 4 Gospels, one book of history, 21 letters to churches and individuals—or 14 Epistles of Paul and 7 General Epistles—and one prophetic book.

The Old Testament was written in the Hebrew language, except that portions of Ezra and Daniel were written in Aramaic. The 27 New Testament books are generally acknowledged to have been written in Greek, the universal language of that time.

The early Bible was written by hand on rolls of papyrus. The Jews later wrote them on leather rolls. The pens were finely-beaten reed brushes, or sharp-pointed reeds; the ink was made from soot, gum, and water.

In some cases the Bible authors did their own writing. In other instances they dictated to scribes (Ex. 24:4; Jer. 36:4).

Up to the fifteenth century copies of the Bible were made by hand.

The Protestant Bible has 66 books, the Catholic 73, and the Jewish 39.

It was not until the fourth century A.D. that the Bible was circulated as one complete volume or unit.

The Bible was divided into chapters in the middle of the thirteenth century by Stephen Langton, Archbishop of Canterbury.

The verse divisions were introduced in 1551 by Robert Stephanus, a Paris publisher of the Greek-Latin edition of the New Testament.

There are more than 4,000 known manuscripts, preserving all or part of the text, dating from about A.D. 200. There are some 8,000 manuscripts of the Latin Vulgate, and at least 1,000 other versions into which the original books were translated.

Early in 1947 the Dead Sea scrolls were discovered. Parts of every book of the Hebrew Old Testament, except Esther, were retrieved from the caves. Probably the most famous find was the Isaiah scroll, found in the first Qumran cave. It is a complete text of the great prophet. The remarkable thing is how closely it resembles the text from which the KJV was made.

David is ascribed as writing 73 of the psalms, but 8 different persons are mentioned as being their authors or compilers. Psalm 90 was written by Moses.

TRANSLATIONS OF THE BIBLE

The Bible has been translated in whole or in part in some 2,000 languages. Today some part of the Bible appears in a new language or dialect about every six weeks.

Greek was the first foreign language into which the Old Testament was translated. This translation, called the Septuagint (often written LXX), is so called because there is a tradition that it was done by seventy men. The work was begun in Alexandria, Egypt, sometime after 285 B.C., and was completed around 130 B.C. This version contains 45 books and was the common Bible of the early Christian church.

The first version of the Bible to be printed was the Latin Vulgate, or "common" version. It was produced by the scholar Jerome, early in the fourth century A.D. This version was based on the Septuagint and translated from the Hebrew, and other ancient versions.

French translations of the Bible were made in the	1100's
Italian and Spanish	1200's
German and English	1300's

In the nineteenth century there were Bibles translated by a physician, an English businessman, and a New England woman, who was the first of her sex to translate the whole Bible. Noah Webster, after writing a successful dictionary, undertook to revise the Bible. It, with the others, was not successful.

Listed below are some versions or translations of the Bible and their dates:

Wycliffe (NT)	1382
Luther's Bible (NT)	1522
(OT)	1534
Tyndale	1525
Coverdale's Bible	1535
Matthew's Bible	1537
The Great Bible	1539
Geneva Bible	1560
Bishop's Bible	1568

26

Douay (Catholic Version)	1609 (Revised, 1763)
King James Version	1611
Revised Version	1885
American Standard Version	1901
Moffatt's Translation (OT)	1913
(NT)	1924
Smith, Goodspeed Version (NT)	1923
(OT)	1927
Ronald Knox (Roman Catholic)	1944
Berkeley	1945
Revised Standard Version	1952
J. B. Phillips (NT)	1957
The Amplified Bible (NT)	1958
(OT)	1964
The New English Bible (NT)	1961
(OT)	1970
The New American Bible (Roman Catholic)	1970
The Living Bible	1971
The New International Version	1978
The Reader's Digest Bible	1982
The New King James	1985
The New Revised Standard Version	1989

More information on some of these Bibles and/or their translations:

WYCLIFFE, JOHN (1382)

Wycliffe's Bible, translated from the Latin Vulgate, was the first extensive rendering of the Scriptures into any form of modern English. It was available only in manuscript copies, making the circulation limited.

LUTHER, MARTIN (1522-1534)

Luther's Bible was a translation into the German language.

TYNDALE, WILLIAM (1525)

Tyndale, a devoted and godly man, has been called the father of the English Bible. He was skilled in seven languages. Eighty per cent of the Old Testament and ninety per cent of the New Testament of his translation is retained in our Authorized Version, a noble monument of his work. It is also estimated that nine tenths of the New Testament in the 1611 King James Bible is his work.

COVERDALE'S BIBLE (1535)

Miles Coverdale's Bible has the distinction of being the first complete English Bible to come from the printing press. Much of the Old Testament and all of the New are largely from Tyndale's Bible, but Coverdale translated the books from Job to Malachi, using the German and Latin as his sources.

MATTHEW'S BIBLE (1537)

Matthew's Bible contained Tyndale's later translations. For the books not translated by Tyndale, the text was taken from Coverdale's version.

THE GREAT BIBLE (1540)

This version was mainly a revision of the text of Matthew's Bible done by Coverdale. Between 1539 and 1541 it appeared in seven editions. Because of its large page size (10 by 15 inches), it was called the Great Bible.

GENEVA VERSION (1560)

The Geneva New Testament appeared in 1557, and the whole Bible in 1560. This edition was published in Geneva, Switzerland, by English religious exiles, and was the first English Bible to divide the chapters into verses. It is considered the most scholarly of the early versions, and because of its popularity, was the Bible used for the next 75 years.

BISHOP'S BIBLE (1568)

Because the English bishops were not pleased with the popularity of the Geneva Bible, they decided to make one of their own. This they did in 1568. This Bible was the second authorized Bible published during the time of Queen Elizabeth. In 1572 it was revised, but it never became popular.

DOUAY-RHEIMS BIBLE (1609)

This Catholic version of the Bible was a direct translation of the Vulgate into English by the Catholic College. The New Testament was issued in 1582 at Rheims, and the Old Testament in 1609 at Douay, France. It was revised in 1763.

KING JAMES VERSION (1611)

This version was prepared by order of England's new king, James I, and was named after him. It took 7 years for the 54 scholars, mostly professors in English universities, to complete this version. One of these men, a chaplain, knew 15 different languages. The youngest of the group was 27 years of age.

No translation has surpassed the literary beauty and popularity of the King James Version. However, like most all revisions, the King James Version was not popular at first, but it was more than two and a half centuries before there were any more major revisions of the English Bible.

REVISED VERSION (1885)

In 1870 plans were made to revise the King James Version. English and American Biblical scholars produced, not a new translation, but a revision of the King James Version, and it was completed in 1885.

AMERICAN STANDARD VERSION (1901)

Certain readings preferred by the American scholars in making the Revised Version, but not included there, were printed in 1901, and called the American Standard Version, or American Revised Version. Though this revision contained improved renderings, it lacked the beauty of language of the King James Version and never became popular with the average Bible reader.

Later this version was revised again and called the Revised Standard Version, or R.S.V. for short.

THE MOFFATT TRANSLATION (1926)

This translation of the Bible by James Moffatt was designed to put the Bible in modern English.

SMITH-GOODSPEED (1923-1931)

This modern-speech translation was prepared with J.M.P. Smith doing the Old Testament, and Edgar J. Goodspeed, of the University of Chicago, doing the New Testament.

KNOX'S VERSION (1944)

This version was the complete Bible translated by Msgr. Ronald A. Knox and based on Latin Vulgate. It was authorized by the Catholic hierarchy of England and Wales.

REVISED STANDARD VERSION (1952)

This Bible was a revision of the American Standard Version, and its acceptance became much wider. However, the King James Version still holds the preeminent place in the hearts of most Bible readers. In 1989 the New Revised Standard Version came out to replace it. It incorporates new understandings gleaned from the Dead Sea scrolls and other manuscript finds.

Thirty-two scholars worked for nearly 20 years to produce this Bible in today's language, and it was completed in 1952.

THE NEW ENGLISH BIBLE (1961)

This Bible was a joint project of the major Protestant bodies of England, the two leading Bible societies, and the Oxford and Cambridge University Presses. The purpose of this new translation was to put the Bible into a clear, understandable English. Right after it came from the presses it was a runaway bestseller and has sold more than a million copies. It has since been revised again under the title *The Revised English Bible* (1989).

THE LIVING BIBLE (1971)

Kenneth Taylor spent 14 years on this work, a paraphrased version of the Bible, prepared especially for young readers in a present-day language that they can understand. This is not recommended as a study Bible.

THE NEW INTERNATIONAL VERSION (1978)

This Bible is a completely new translation, taken directly from the best available Hebrew, Aramaic, and Greek texts. It was the aim of the more than 100 scholars to produce a Bible in the contemporary language of our day. It began in 1965 and in 1973 the New Testament was published. The entire Bible was printed in 1978. Additional revisions were made in 1983 and appear in printings after that date.

THE READER'S DIGEST BIBLE (1982)

A committee of 8 editors worked nonstop for 3 years to prepare the first true condensation of the Bible, slashing a third of a million words from the original version on which it was based (the RSV). The Old Testament was cut 50%, and the New 25%. Genesis was cut 53%; Exodus 58%; Daniel 59% — (ending with Daniel 7); Isaiah 61%; Hebrews 46%; and Revelation 22%. Of the original 150 psalms, only 79 remain. Psalm 23 is now Psalm 13.

This Bible was given the title "The Holey Bible," referring to the holes that were left when so much was taken out.

THE NEW KING JAMES (1985)

This version was the fifth major revision of the original Authorized Version in over 300 years. Over 130 deeply committed Christian scholars spent seven years and over $4 million to complete this privately-funded project. They were deeply committed to preserve the revered KJV, but to put it in more understandable language. An interesting note is that the initial translation of 1611 also took 7 years to produce.

30

THE PRINTING OF THE BIBLE

Johannes Gutenberg produced the first printed Bible in 1455. It later sold to the Library of Congress for $350,000.

The first complete English Bible was by Wycliffe and his followers and appeared in England in 1382.

The first Bible was printed in America in 1663. It was a translation into the Mohican language by John Eliot, missionary to the Indians.

The smallest Bible reported to have been printed is the entire Bible reduced to a two-inch square Microform which can be read on a microfilm reader.

Into the production of the Revised Standard Version, went 2,000 gallons of ink, 1,000 tons of paper, 10 tons of type metal, 71 miles of 40-inch cloth, and enough 23-karat gold leaf, for stamping the name, to pave a road 24 feet wide and a mile long. The finished books, stacked in one pile, would reach higher than 100 Empire State Buildings. This first printing alone cost about $6 million.

The "Thumb Bible" was printed in Scotland in 1670. It was one inch square and ½ inch thick.

The American Bible Society has distributed about 900 million Bibles and parts of the Bible since its beginning in 1816.

Some mistakes made in printing the Bible were:

1631. An edition of the King James Bible had the word *not* left out of the seventh commandment, making it read: "Thou shalt commit adultery." The printer was fined 300 francs for this mistake. In an earlier edition one verse used the word *Judas* instead of *Jesus*, and another verse was printed twice.

1717. The "Vinegar Bible." The headline of Luke 20 read "The parable of the vinegar" instead of "The parable of the vineyard."

1549. The "Wife-Beater Bible." This Bible reads in 1 Peter that husbands should "beat the fear of God" into their wives' heads.

31

1551. The "Bug Bible." A Bible was printed in which Psalm 91:5 read "Thou shalt not be afraid of any bugs by night." The King James Version reads "terror by night."

1638. The "Forgotten Sins Bible." Typesetters changed "forgiven" to "forgotten" in Luke 7:47, reading: "Her sins, which are many, are forgotten."

1653. John Field, a publisher, left out a "not" in 1 Cor. 6:9 saying: "Know ye that the unrighteous shall inherit the kingdom of God?"

1702. A version appeared that spoke of David as being persecuted by "printers" instead of "princes" in Psalm 119:161.

1716. The "Sin On Bible." This first English Bible to be printed in Ireland has Isaiah as saying, "Sin on more."

1801. A Bible in which the word *murderers* was used instead of *murmurers* in Jude 16.

1801. The "Murderers Bible." This Bible's third edition has "killed" instead of "filled" in Mark 7:27, saying, "Let the children first be killed."

1810. The "Wife-hater Bible." This Bible was printed using the word "wife" instead of "life" in Luke 14:26. It became known as the "wife-hater" Bible. Also that year in Matthew 13:43 it was printed "ears to ear" instead of "ears to hear."

1823. "The Camels Bible." In this Bible Rebekah is said to have left her tent with her entourage of "camels," instead of "damsels." Thus it was called "The Camels Bible."

A wrong letter in an Eskimo translation turned "nation shall rise against nation" (Matt. 24:7) into "a pair of snowshoes shall rise up against a pair of snowshoes."

FACTS AND FIGURES
ABOUT THE BIBLE

The Bible contains: 3,566,480 letters
773,742 words
31,173 verses
1,189 chapters
66 books

Numbers 7 is the second longest chapter of the Bible with 89 verses and 1,939 words. In this chapter 4 different verses are repeated at intervals about 10 times.

There are 929 chapters in the Old Testament, and 260 in the New, totaling 1,189.

There are 39 books in the Old Testament. Multiply one digit by the other and you will have the number of books in the New Testament, 27.

You can read the Bible through in one year if you read 3 chapters a day each weekday and read 5 chapters every weekend.

THE MIDDLE, THE LONGEST, THE SHORTEST

The longest chapter:	Psalm 119, with 176 verses.
The shortest chapter:	Psalm 117, with 2 verses, 33 words.
The longest verse, OT:	Esther 8:9, with 90 words, or 426 letters.
The longest verse, NT:	Rev. 20:4, with 68 words, 284 letters.
The shortest verse:	John 11:35, with 9 letters.
The shortest book of the Bible:	Obadiah.
The shortest book, OT:	Obadiah.
The shortest book, NT:	2 John.
The shortest verse, OT:	1 Chronicles 1:25.
The shortest chapter, NT:	Revelation 15.
The middle chapter of the Bible:	Psalm 117.
The middle chapter, OT:	Job 29
The middle chapter, NT:	Romans 13.
The middle book of the Bible:	Micah.
The middle book, OT:	Proverbs.
The middle book, NT:	2 Thessalonians.
The middle verse of the Bible:	Psalm 103:2.
The middle verse, OT:	2 Chronicles 20:18.
The middle verse, NT:	Acts 17:17.

POTPOURRI

All but two of the 176 verses in Psalm 119 make reference to the Scriptures in some way. David Livingstone could quote this entire chapter at the age of 9 with only 3 mistakes.

Psalm 119 is what is called an acrostic. It has 176 verses, divided into 22 sections of eight verses each. In the Hebrew the first group of verses begins with the first letter of the Hebrew alphabet, which is Aleph, or A, the second with the second letter, which is Beth, or B, and so on. It does not show in the English translation, but if you notice the strange words or letters printed between each two sections in some Bibles you will see the letters and their names. Copy the letters in order, and you will be writing the Hebrew alphabet.

Ninety-five per cent, or 600 verses, of Mark appear in Matthew. One half of Mark appears in Luke.

It has been estimated that the word *and* occurs in the Bible 46,219 times. The word *Jehovah* appears 6,823 times.

The word *reverend* appears in the Bible only once; it applies to God.

By one estimate the Bible has 406 references to "blood."

The two words *fear not* are said to be repeated 74 times in the Bible.

By one count, the Bible contains 7,487 promises that God has made to man. There are estimated to be some 8,810 promises of all kinds in the Bible.

The Old Testament is more than 3 times as long as the New Testament.

It is said that there have been 10,000 decrees of kings and princes to destroy the Bible, but it still lives.

There are only 24 verses in Mark that aren't either in Matthew or Luke.

By one count there are about 260 direct quotations from the

Old Testament in the New Testament. Some of those cited are:

    Genesis, quoted 19 times in 9 New Testament books
    Exodus, 24 times in 12 NT books
    Numbers, quoted or alluded to in 9 NT books
    Deuteronomy, 26 times in 13 NT books
    Psalms, 59 times in 12 NT books
    Isaiah, 50 times in 11 NT books
    Proverbs, 6 times in 6 NT books
    Zechariah, 6 times in 4 NT books

There are quotations in the New Testament from the Old Testament from every book except Judges, Ezra, Nehemiah, Esther, Ecclesiastes, and the Song of Solomon.

There are 404 verses in the book of Revelation, with about 550 references made to Old Testament passages.

There are only 3 chapters in the entire Bible, excluding Psalm 119, with 80 or more verses. They are: Numbers 7, I Chronicles 6 and Luke 1.

There are 5 books of the Bible with only 1 chapter. They are: Jude, Obadiah, Philemon and I and II John.

Esther and the Song of Solomon are the only books of the Bible that do not mention the word *God* or *Lord*.

Isaiah 8:1 has the longest word in the entire Bible, "Mahershalalhashbaz."

2 Kings 19 and Isaiah 37 are almost identical.

Luke is the only Gospel writer who recorded the childhood of Jesus.

Hebrews 12:21 records a saying of Moses not found in the Old Testament.

Acts 13:33 is a quotation in the New Testament that tells exactly from where it is taken in the Old Testament.

Numbers 21:17, 18 is the shortest song recorded in the Bible.

Ezra 7:21 contains all the letters of the alphabet but J.

1 Chron. 12:40 contains all the letters of the alphabet but Q.

2 Timothy 1:5 is the only place where the word *grandmother* appears in the Bible.

The Old Testament ends with a curse. The New Testament ends with a blessing.

"Jesus Christ" appears in the first and last verse of the New Testament.

Twenty-four of the twenty-seven books of the New Testament end in "Amen."

Psalm 136. Every verse in this chapter ends with the same words.

Song of Solomon 2:1. This verse refers to a rose and a lily. By one count the Bible mentions 116 different types of shrubs, plants and flowers.

Psalm 103. No passage of equal length in the entire Bible contains so exalted and comprehensive a description of the character of God as this one.

Ecclesiastes 12 mentions the following items: sun, moon, stars, clouds, birds, grasshopper, house, windows, doors, streets, tree, men, bowl and pitcher.

Leviticus 25:10. Part of this verse is inscribed on the Liberty Bell in Independence Hall, Philadelphia.

Acts 21:40 is a chapter that does not end in a period.

"Thus saith the Lord," and "God said," is estimated to occur more than 2,500 times in the Bible.

The expression "The Lord spake," "God said," and similar expressions are said to be found more than 500 times in the first 5 books of the Bible.

Psalm 23, Isaiah 35, Micah 6, 1 Corinthians 13 and Revelation 21, all in the King James Version, find no parallel in English literature as far as style and beauty of expression is concerned.

Some interesting Bible texts:

Proverbs 11:22 — "As a jewel of gold in a swine's snout."
Job 19:20 — "I am escaped with the skin of my teeth."
Numbers 32:23 — "be sure your sin will find you out."
Ecclesiastes 5:12 — "The sleep of a labouring man is sweet, whether he eat little or much."
Proverbs 25:19 — "Confidence in an unfaithful man . . . is like a broken tooth, and a foot out of joint."
Job 8:9 — "For we are but of yesterday, and know nothing."
Proverbs 24:13 — "My son, eat thou honey, because it is good."
Proverbs 25:27 — "It is not good to eat much honey."

Some interesting Bible phrases:

Deuteronomy 32:10 — "Apple of his eye."
Romans 13:1 — "Powers that be."
Luke 10:7 — "Worthy of his hire."
Revelation 22:1 — "Clear as crystal."
2 Corinthians 12:7 — "Thorn in the flesh."
Matthew 5:13 — "Salt of the earth."
1 Peter 5:2 — "Filthy lucre."
Matthew 7:6 — "Pearls before swine."
Matthew 8:20 — "Birds of the air."
1 Kings 19:12 — "Still small voice."
Isaiah 53:7 — "As a lamb to the slaughter."
Proverbs 25:11 — "A word fitly spoken."
Matthew 5:38 — "An eye for an eye."

FASCINATING BIBLICAL WORDS

APOCALYPSE – A transliteration of the Greek name of the book of Revelation.

ARMAGEDDON – A cryptic designation for the battlefield of "The battle of that great day of God Almighty" (Rev. 16:14, 16).

BOTCH (Deut. 28:27) – An eruption of the skin, a boil.

CARBUNCLE (Ex. 28:17) – A precious stone; one of these was used in the high priest's breastplate.

COCKATRICE (Isa. 14:29) – A poisonous snake.

FULLER   (Mark 9:3) – A cleaner and bleacher of garments.

GIN (Amos 3:5) – A snare to catch birds.

OBEISANCE (Gen. 37:7) – Bowing down.

PULSE (Dan. 1:12) – Food derived from plants, such as cereals, vegetables, berries, and dates.

SACKBUT (Dan. 3:5) – An incorrect rendering in the K.J.V. of a word referring to a 4-stringed instrument. A sackbut was actually a medieval wind instrument.

SANHEDRIN – In the time of Christ, the chief Jewish judicial body, composed of 71 members.

TITTLE (Matt. 5:18) – A small projection or ornamental hook on a letter.

MONEY AND WEIGHTS

The use of coined money was apparently unknown before the seventh or eighth century B.C. It was first introduced in Lydia, in Asia Minor, at that time. Prior to that, trading was done by the bartering of animals and agricultural products and by exchange of metals, which were weighed. The earliest mention of a sale of property in the Bible is Abraham's purchase of a burial cave at Machpelah, for which he weighed four hundred shekels of silver as payment (Gen. 23:16).

ASSARION — A small Roman copper coin worth about one cent. It is translated "farthing" in the King James Version (Matt. 10:29; Luke 12:6).

BEKAH — A Hebrew weight equivalent to 5.7 grams (Ex. 38:26).

DENARIUS or PENNY (K.J.V.) — A silver Roman coin originally worth about 18 cents, but later devalued to about 8 cents. It was equivalent of a day's wages and therefore of a higher value than its weight (Matt. 20:2, 9, 10, 13; Luke 10:35; John 6:7, etc.).

DRAM — In the K.J.V. the translation of two Hebrew terms referring to a Hebrew silver coin (Ezra 2:69; Neh. 7:70-72); and a Persian coin (1 Chron. 29:7; Ezra 8:27) worth about $5.00.

MITE — Smallest copper coin used in Christ's time, worth about 1/8th of a cent. Equivalent to a half farthing (Mark 12:42; Luke 21:2).

GERAH — The smallest weight, 1/20th of a shekel (Lev. 27:25; Num. 3:47; Eze. 45:12).

POUND — Equal to 100 silver drachma. Its value was about $10.50 (Luke 19:13-25).

SHEKEL — A weight used in financial transactions anciently (Gen. 24:22). Coins began to replace it in the seventh century B.C.

SILVERLING — A piece of silver mentioned only once (Isa. 7:23) in the K.J.V. and R.S.V.

TALENT – Largest weight used for metals by the ancients (2 Kings 23:33; Matt. 25:14-30). It consisted of about 3,000 shekels.

PIM – Equal to about two thirds of a shekel, or 0.268 ounce (1 Sam. 13:19-21).

DRY MEASURES

CAB or KAB – Equivalent to 1/11 dry quart (2 Kings 6:25).

TENTH DEAL – Equivalent to an omer, about 2 quarts (Ex. 29: 40; Lev. 14:41; Num. 28:13).

OMER – Same as a tenth deal.

MEASURE – Translation of the Hebrew *Se'ah*, the equivalent of about 1/5 U.S. bushel (1 Sam. 25:18; 2 Kings 7:16, 18).

EPHAH – The Hebrew measurement equalled 5.8 gallons, the same as a bath (Ex. 16:36; Judges 6:19).

HOMER – Not to be confused with the omer. Ten ephahs, or about 6¼ U.S. bushels (Lev. 27:16; Num. 11:32; Eze. 45:11).

LIQUID MEASURES

LOG – A little less than 1/3 quart; about 1 1/3 cups (Lev. 14: 10).

HIN – A measure of Egyptian origin equal to about 3.87 U.S. quarts (Ex. 29:40; 30:24; Num. 15:4-9; Eze. 4:11).

BATH – One of the larger liquid measures of Biblical times, equal to 6 hins and equivalent to about 5.8 U.S. gallons (1 Kings 7:26; Eze. 45:11).

FIRKIN – Estimated to be about 10 gallons (John 2:6).

COR – The equivalent of about 58 U.S. gallons, or about the same as a homer (Eze. 45:14).

POUND – Between 11 and 12 ounces in our weight (John 19:39).

LINEAL MEASURES

CUBIT — The Hebrew cubit (Deut. 3:11, etc.) was about 17½ inches long. The "long cubit" (Eze. 40:5, R.S.V.) was about 20 inches long. In Mesopotamia the cubit was 19 inches.

FINGER — The breadth of a man's finger, or about .73 inch (Jer. 52:21).

HANDBREADTH — The width of the hand, either 2.92 inches (Hebrew) or 3.42 inches (Egyptian) (Ex. 37:12; 1 Kings 7:26; 2 Chron. 4:5; Ps. 39:5).

SPAN — Three handbreadths — 8.75 inches long (Hebrew) or 10.3 inches (Egyptian) (Ex. 28:16; 39:9; 1 Sam. 17:4).

FATHOM — Equivalent to 6 feet (Acts 27:28).

MEASURING REED — Ezekiel's reed (Eze. 40:3, 5) was that of an old measurement, which made it 12 feet long.

FURLONG — This Greek *stadion* was adopted by the Jews. It measured 600 Greek feet, 25 Roman feet, and about 606 English feet. Emmaus was about 60 *stadia*, or 7 miles, from Jerusalem (Luke 24:13).

MILE — The Roman mile was 8 stadia, or about 4,855 feet (Matt. 5:41).

SABBATH DAY'S JOURNEY — The exact length of this distance uncertain. Josephus states that it is 5 or 6 stadia, or between 3,000 and 3,600 feet. This is approximately the distance from Jerusalem to the Mount of Olives (Acts 1:12).

DAY'S JOURNEY — In Bible times the distance was usually measured by the length of time necessary to travel: e.g. "three days' journey" (Ex. 3:18), "seven days' journey" (Gen. 31:23). In NT times the distance was measured in furlongs or Roman miles (Luke 24:13; Matt. 5:41).

AREA MEASURE — The OT term translated acre (1 Sam. 14:14; Isa. 5:10) was an area that a team of oxen could plow in one day. This has been estimated at about ½ U.S. acre.

HOLY LAND DISTANCES

From Jerusalem to Jericho is 15 miles.

From Dan to Beersheba, by air, is 125 miles.

The Jordan River is 180 yards wide and 3 feet deep at its
mouth.

The Sea of Galilee is 13 miles long and is 6 miles broad at its
widest.

DID YOU KNOW THAT . . .?

Leviticus 13:40 is a text atheists can't deny.

2 Kings 21:13 tells the way a person wipes a dish.

2 Samuel 21:20 and 1 Chronicles 20:6 tell of a man with 24 fingers and toes.

2 Chronicles 11:21 tells of a man with 88 children. He had 18 wives, and 60 concubines.

Judges 12:5, 6 tells of men who were slain because they couldn't pronounce a word correctly.

Job 39:19, 25 describes a horse, as saying, "Ha, ha."

Judges 20:16 refers to 700 Benjamites who were left-handed and especially skillful in a certain practice.

Proverbs 20:29 tells us what the glory of young men is, and what the beauty of old men is.

Job 26:7 says that the earth hangs upon nothing.

1 Kings 19:4-8 describes an angel's providing two meals.

2 Samuel 20:9 tells how a soldier took hold of another to kiss him.

Genesis 41:14 has the first Bible reference to shaving.

Deuteronomy 29:5 tells how long the Israelites wore the same shoes and clothes.

Isaiah 22:18 suggests that ball-playing is a very ancient sport.

Ezekiel 16:4 tells us that anciently new-born babies were salted.

Ezekiel 23:6 tells us that certain soldiers wore blue, or purple (R.S.V.) uniforms.

Job 6:6, (K.J.V.), says that the white of an egg is tasteless.

Proverbs 30:33 indicates that anciently butter was churned.

Deuteronomy 20:1, 28 tells that cowards were exempt from military service in the ancient Jewish army.

Deuteronomy 6:7 and Deuteronomy 11:19, K.J.V., are two verses exactly alike.

1 Samuel 13:19 tells us that at a certain time there were no blacksmiths in Israel.

Mark 15:36 has the only mention of a sponge in the Bible.

Judges 9:7-15 is a parable of trees talking.

2 Kings 10:8 speaks of two heaps of heads at a city gate.

2 Chronicles 30:18 is a verse ending without punctuation.

Nehemiah 8:4 is the only Biblical reference to the usage of a pulpit.

2 Samuel 19:18, K.J.V., speaks of a ferry boat.

John 1 has been called the "finders" chapter. John found Jesus, Andrew found Peter, Jesus found Philip, and Philip found Nathaniel.

Mark 6:3 mentions Jesus' family.

Judges 3:17 refers to a very fat man.

Acts 7:23 refers to Moses' age at a certain time, information that is not in the OT.

Leviticus 24:10-12, 23 records the stoning of a man who blasphemed the name of the Lord, and cursed.

Deuteronomy 34:7 and Joshua 14:11 tell of two Hebrew leaders whose strength did not abate with old age.

The Word of God is likened to:

A fire	—	Jer. 23:29
A lamp	—	Ps. 119:105
A sword	—	Eph. 6:17
A two-edged sword	—	Heb. 4:12
Milk	—	1 Peter 2:2
Food	—	Jer. 15:16
Seed	—	Luke 8:11
A hammer	—	Jer. 23:29

About 400 years passed from the time of Nehemiah and the prophet Malachi to New Testament times. No prophet spoke or wrote during that "period of silence."

Job is thought by some to be the oldest book of the Bible.

The word *lamb* is used 29 times in Revelation, and only once elsewhere in the entire New Testament, and John himself is the one using it in John 21:15.

Seventeen of the 66 books of the Bible are at least partly prophetic in nature, and many passages in the other books contain prophetic statements.

By one count the Bible makes predictions on 737 subjects. It has been estimated that there are approximately 8,352 "predictive verses" in the Old and New Testaments.

Twenty-seven per cent of the entire Bible is said to be predictive in nature. Estimated another way, 28.5 per cent of the Old Testament and 21.5 per cent of the New Testament is prophecy.

In terms of the total number of verses, it has been estimated that Ezekiel has the most prophetic verses, 821, in the Old Testament. By the same scale Matthew, with 278 such verses, has the most predictive material of any New Testament book.

There is no predictive matter in Ruth, the Song of Solomon, Philemon, and 3 John.

By one estimate, one verse in every ten in the Bible speaks directly or indirectly of the second coming of Christ.

In the Bible in one form or another we are solemnly charged more than 160 times to care for the poor.

One of the longest chapters in the Bible is Numbers 7 — and it is all about giving.

The word *Calvary* is mentioned only once in the Bible, in Luke 23:33.

With its prophecies the book of Revelation also has its music. The words of seven anthems are recorded there, as well as other singing.

Elisha is the only man recorded in connection with whom a miracle took place after his death (2 Kings 13:20).

It is estimated that in the life of Joseph there are more than 100 parallels to the life of Christ, and that, while he, like ourselves, had faults they are not recorded.

The events recorded in Genesis closed some 300 years before Moses was born, thus the information he received to write this book came from God, or was passed along from his fore-fathers.

Christ quotes from 22 Old Testament books.

Although the book of Esther follows Nehemiah, the events chronicled there took place 30 years before those recorded in Nehemiah.

There are said to be 17 incidents in the Bible that refer to Jesus' keeping the Sabbath.

The New Jerusalem, according to Revelation 21:16, measures 12,000 stadia (R.S.V.). It is not clear whether this measure-ment is of one side or the circumference. It is usually under-stood as referring to the circumference, which would be about 1,378.4 miles around. One side would be about 344.6 miles. The city's area would be approximately 118,749 square miles, which is larger than the combined area of North Carolina, Virginia, and West Virginia. The city has a wall of jasper 210 feet high, 12 foundations of 12 precious stones, 12 gates, each one of one solid pearl, streets of gold, and mansions of gold for the saints.

The book of Isaiah has been likened to a miniature Bible. It has 66 chapters; the Bible has 66 books. It has 2 major divisions like the Bible. The first division comes after chapter 39; the Bible has 39 books in the OT. The second division has 27 books; the NT has 27 books.

The OT opens with man and sin; Isaiah opens with man and sin. Almost the last part of the first section of Isaiah (chapter 34, 35) deals with prophecies of the coming King and the redemption of God's people; the last part of the OT predicts His coming kingdom.

The second part of Isaiah begins with "the voice of him that crieth in the wilderness" (chap. 40:3), just as, early in the NT, John the Baptist, the forerunner of Jesus, is introduced.

Both Isaiah and the NT end with the visions of the new heavens and new earth (Isa. 65, 66; Rev. 21, 22).

USES OF THE BIBLE

FOR MEDITATION — Ps. 119:97-99
"O how I love thy law! It is my meditation all the day . . . .
I have more understanding than all my teachers: for thy testimonies are my meditation."

FOR ADMONITION — 1 Cor. 10:11
"Now all these things . . . are written for our admonition."

FOR LIGHT — Ps. 119:105, 130
"Thy word is a lamp unto my feet, and a light unto my path."
"The entrance of thy words giveth light; it giveth understanding unto the simple."

FOR CLEANSING — Ps. 119:9
"Wherewithal shall a young man cleanse his way? By taking heed thereto according to thy word."

FOR JOY — Ps. 119:14, 24, 162
"I have rejoiced in the way of thy testimonies, as much as in all riches." "Thy testimonies also are my delight." "I rejoice at thy word."

FOR STRENGTH — Ps. 119:28
"My soul melteth for heaviness: strengthen thou me according unto thy word."

FOR TRUST — Ps. 119:42
"So shall I have wherewith to answer him that reproacheth me: for I trust in thy word."

FOR PEACE — Ps. 119:165
"Great peace have they which love thy law; and nothing shall offend them."

FOR BELIEF — John 20:31
"But these are written, that ye might believe."

FOR INSTRUCTION — 2 Tim. 3:16
" All scripture is given by inspiration of God, and is profitable for doctrine, for reproof, for correction, for instruction in righteousness."

IMPORTANT
CHAPTERS OF THE BIBLE

Backsliding	Jeremiah 3
Baptism	Romans 6
Beatitudes	Matthew 5
Birth and childhood of Jesus	Luke 2
Bread of life	John 6
Capital and labor	James 5
Christian living	Romans 12-14
Cross, psalm of	Psalm 22
Crucifixion	John 19
Death	Job 14; Psalm 146
Destruction of wicked	Psalm 37; Malachi 4
Faith chapter	Hebrews 11
Forgiveness, prayer for	Psalms 32, 51
God's character	Psalm 103
God's church	Ephesians 4
God's final warning messages	Revelation 14
Good Shepherd	Ezekiel 34; John 10
Good wife and mother	Proverbs 31
Harvest Psalm	Psalm 65
Hope chapter	Psalm 71
Holy Spirit	John 14
Judging	Romans 2
Last days	2 Timothy 3
Latter Rain, preparation for	Joel 2
Lord's Prayer	Matthew 6 (verses 9-13)
Lord's Prayer (for disciples)	John 17
Lord's Supper	Matthew 26 (verses 26-30); 1 Corinthians 11 (verses 23-30)
Love chapter	1 Corinthians 13
Love-of-God	1 John 4
Marriage	1 Corinthians 7; Ephesians 5
Meats, clean and unclean	Leviticus 11; Deuteronomy 14
Millennium	Revelation 20

TWENTY FAVORITE
SHORT STORIES

1.	Joseph	Genesis 37, 39-48
2.	Moses in the bulrushes	Exodus 2
3.	Balaam and Balak	Numbers 22-24
4.	Capture of Jericho	Joshua 6
5.	Gideon and the 300 men	Judges 7
6.	Samson	Judges 14-16
7.	Ruth	Book of Ruth
8.	David and Goliath	1 Samuel 17
9.	David and Jonathan	1 Samuel 18-20
10.	Elijah and the Prophets of Baal	1 Kings 18
11.	Naboth's vineyard	1 Kings 21
12.	The ascension of Elijah	2 Kings 2
13.	Queen Esther	Book of Esther
14.	The fiery furnace	Daniel 3
15.	Daniel in the lions' den	Daniel 6
16.	Jonah	Book of Jonah
17.	The good Samaritan	Luke 10:25-37
18.	The prodigal son	Luke 15:11-32
19.	Healing of the lame man	John 5:1-9
20.	Shipwreck of Paul	Acts 27

NUMBERS IN THE BIBLE

By one estimate the number 7 is used 230 times in the Old and New Testament.

Some of the uses of 7:

God rested on seventh day after six days of Creation (Gen. 2:2, 3; Ex. 20:8-11).

Enoch the seventh from Adam (Jude 14).

Clean beasts went into the ark by sevens (Gen. 7:2).

Door of ark closed 7 days before Flood (Gen. 7:9, 10).

Number of years Jacob worked, twice, for Rachel (Gen. 29:18-28).

Pharaoh dreamed of 7 lean and 7 fat cows (Gen. 41:17-21).

Waters of Egypt were blood 7 days (Gen. 7:20, 25).

Times Jericho was marched around on day walls fell (Joshua 6:4).

Numer of locks of hair Delilah shaved from Samson's head (Judges 16:19).

Years it took for Solomon to build the Temple (1 Kings 6:38).

Shunammite's son when raised to life sneezed 7 times (2 Kings 4:35).

Naaman washed 7 times in Jordan (2 Kings 5:9-14).

Nebuchadnezzar dwelt among beasts 7 years (Dan. 4:13-17, 28-34).

Number of baskets of fragments left after feeding 4,000 (Matt. 15:37).

Seven loaves and a few fishes to feed the 4,000 men, besides the women and children (Matt. 15:34-36).

Number of devils Jesus cast out of Mary Magdalene (Mark 16:9).

Seven stars (Rev. 1:16).

Seven churches (Rev. 1:4, 11, 20).

Seven seals (Rev. 8:1).

Seven trumpets (Rev. 8:2-8).

Seven thunders (Rev. 10:3, 4).

The 7 last plagues (Rev. 15,16).

Seven deacons in early church (Acts 6:3-5).

NAMES IN THE BIBLE

More than 250 names are given for God in the Bible.

The word Lord occurs 1,853 times in the Bible.

The word Jehovah occurs 5,845 times.

There are 3,340 people named in the Bible.

Moses is the most frequently mentioned Old Testament figure in the New Testament.

David is mentioned 860 times in the Bible, which is more than any other name. Moses is the second most often named.

The name of Moses is mentioned in 32 different books of the Bible; David in 29 books. Abraham is mentioned in 26; Isaiah 20.

Jesus, Paul, and Peter are the most mentioned men in the New Testament.

The most often mentioned woman's name in the Bible is Sarah; Rachel is second.

Mary Magdalene is the most frequently named woman in the New Testament.

There are more than 100 names in the Bible beginning with the letter A; more than 60 with J; 50 with S; and 40 with M.

There are 21 with the name of Meshullom and 13 with Jonathan.

Anna, Hannah, and Eve are three Bible names which are the same spelled backward or forward.

BIBLE FIRSTS

First thing to be created — light (Gen. 1:3).

First recorded words spoken to man — "Be fruitful . . ." (Gen. 1:28).

First lie — "Ye shall not surely die" (Gen. 3:4).

First murderer — Cain (Gen. 4:8).

First city built — Enoch (Gen. 4:17).

First recorded tentmaker — Jabal (Gen. 4:20).

First musician — Jubal (Gen. 4:21).

First mentioned worker in iron and brass — Tubal-cain (Gen. 4:22).

First recorded man to die a natural death — Adam (Gen. 5:5).

First mountain mentioned — Aarat (Gen. 8:4).

First Biblical mention of weeping — Hagar (Gen. 21:16).

First recorded twins — Jacob and Esau (Gen. 25:23-26).

First judge mentioned — Moses (Ex. 18:13).

First high priest mentioned — Aaron (Ex. 28:1).

First king of Israel — Saul (1 Sam. 11:15).

First miracle of Christ—water to wine (John 2:1-11).

First disciple called by Jesus — Simon Peter (Matt. 4:18, 19).

First Christian martyr — Stephen (Acts 7:58-59).

First Christian missionaries — Paul and Barnabas (Acts 13:2-4).

First person to see Jesus after resurrection — Mary Magdalene (Mark 16:9).

PROPHECIES CONCERNING JESUS

PROPHECY	PROPHESIED	FULFILLED
Birthplace	Micah 5:2	Matt. 2:1,6
Mother	Isa. 7:14	Matt. 1:18-23
Tribe	Gen. 49:10	Heb. 7:14
His work	Isa. 61:1-3	Luke 4:16-21
A healer	Isa. 53:4	Matt. 8:16,17
Teach in parables	Ps. 78:2	Matt. 13:34,35
Triumphant entry	Zech. 9:9	Matt. 21:1-11
Betrayer	Ps. 41:9	John 13:18,19 26
Price sold for	Zech. 11:12	Matt. 26:14-16
How money used	Zech. 11:13	Matt. 27:3-8
Disciples forsake	Zech. 13:7	Matt. 26:31
Spit upon	Isa. 50:6	Matt. 26:67
Smitten with rod	Micah 5:1	Matt. 27:30
Silence in persecution	Isa. 53:7	Matt. 27:12-14
Manner of death	Zech. 12:10	John 19:18, 34-37
Location of wounds	Ps. 22:16	John 20:25
Taunting words	Ps. 22:7, 8	Matt. 27:39, 41-44
With criminals	Isa. 53:9, 12	Mark 15:27,28
Agonizing cry	Ps. 22:1	Matt. 27:46
Prayer for enemies	Isa. 53:12	Luke 23:34
Drink offered	Ps. 69:21	John 19:28-30
Garments	Ps. 22:18	John 19:23,24
No bones broken	Ps. 34:20	John 19:36
His burial	Isa. 53:9	Matt. 27: 57-60
His resurrection	Ps. 16:10	Acts 2:30, 31
His ascension	Ps. 24:7-10	1 Peter 3:22

TITLES OF CHRIST
IN THE BIBLE

OLD TESTAMENT

Seed of the Woman	Gen. 3:15
A Star Out of Jacob	Num. 24:17
A Prophet	Deut. 18:15, 18
The Mighty God	Isa. 9:6
The Everlasting Father	Isa. 9:6
The Prince of Peace	Isa. 9:6
The Lord Our Righteousness	Jer. 23:6
The Son of God	Dan. 3:25
The Son of Man	Dan. 7:13
Michael, the Great Prince	Dan. 12:1
The Branch	Zech. 6:12
The Sun of Righteousness	Mal. 4:2

NEW TESTAMENT

The Word	John 1:1
The Lamb of God	John 1:29
The Bread of Life	John 6:35
The Light of the World	John 8:12
The Door of the Sheep	John 10:7
The Good Shepherd	John 10:11
The Resurrection and the Life	John 11:25
The Way, the Truth, and the Life	John 14:6
The True Vine	John 15:1
The Rock	1 Cor. 10:4
The Second Adam	1 Cor. 15:45, 47
The Chief Cornerstone	Eph. 2:20
A Great High Priest	Heb. 4:14
The Chief Shepherd	1 Peter 5:4
An Advocate	1 John 2:1
Michael the Archangel	Jude 9
King of Kings	Rev. 19:16
Lord of Lords	Rev. 19:16
The Morning Star	Rev. 22:16

CHRIST'S SEVEN "WORDS" ON THE CROSS

1. "Father, forgive them; for they know not what they do." Luke 23:34.

2. "Verily I say unto thee this day: With me shalt thou be in Paradise." Luke 23:43, Rotherham.

3. "Woman, behold thy son!" "Behold thy mother!" John 19: 26, 27.

4. "My God, my God, why hast thou forsaken me?" Matt. 27: 46.

5. "I thirst." John 19:28.

6. "It is finished." John 19:30.

7. "Father, into thy hands I commend my spirit." Luke 23:46.

PARABLES OF JESUS

Houses on rock and sand	Matt. 7:24-27
New cloth, old garments	Matt. 9:16
New wine, old bottles	Matt. 9:17
Sower	Matt. 13:3-9
Tares	Matt. 13:24-30, 36-43
Seed growing untended	Mark 4:26-29
Householder and servants	Mark 13:34-37
Grain of mustard seed	Matt. 13:31, 32
Leaven	Matt. 13:33
Hid treasure	Matt. 13:44
Precious pearl	Matt. 13:45, 46
Draw-net	Matt. 13:47-50
Householder and treasure	Matt. 13:52
Two debtors	Luke 7:40-47
Unmerciful servant	Matt. 18:23-35
Good Samaritan	Luke 10:25-37
Friend at midnight	Luke 11:5-13
Rich fool	Luke 12:16-21
The waiting servants	Luke 12:35-48
Barren fig tree	Luke 13:6-9
Seats at a feast	Luke 14:7-11
Great supper	Luke 14:15-24
Tower; king contemplating war	Luke 14:28-33
Lost sheep	Luke 15:3-7
Lost piece of money	Luke 15:8-10
Prodigal son	Luke 15:11-32
Unjust steward	Luke 16:1-12
Rich man and Lazarus	Luke 16:19-31
Unprofitable servant	Luke 17:7-10
The persistent widow	Luke 18:1-8
Pharisee and publican	Luke 18:9-14
Laborers in the vineyard	Matt. 20:1-16
Pounds	Luke 19:11-27
Two sons	Matt. 21:28-32
Wicked husbandmen	Matt. 21:33-43
Marriage of king's son	Matt. 22:1-14
Fig tree	Matt. 24:32, 33
Ten virgins	Matt. 25:1-13
Ten talents	Matt. 25:14-30
Sheep and goats	Matt. 25:31-46

MIRACLES OF JESUS

Water turned to wine	John 2:1-11
Nobleman's son cured	John 4:45-54
Healed invalid at Bethesda	John 5:1-15
Miraculous draught of fishes	Luke 5:1-11
Demoniac at Capernaum cured	Mark 1:21-28
Healed Peter's wife's mother	Mark 1:29-31
Healed leper at Capernaum	Mark 1:40-45
Paralytic cured	Mark 2:1-12
Restored withered hand	Mark 3:1-6
Healed centurion's servant	Matt. 8:5-13
Sight restored to two blind men	Matt. 9:27-31
Dumb Demoniac healed	Matt. 9:32-34
Raised son of widow of Nain	Luke 7:11-17
Blind, dumb demoniac healed	Matt. 12:22-32
Calmed storm on Galilee	Matt. 8:23-27
Cured demoniacs of Gadara	Matt. 8:28-34
Cured a woman of a bloody flux	Luke 8:43-48
Restored life to Jairus' daughter	Matt. 9:18-26
Fed the 5,000	Matt. 14:15-21
Jesus walked on water	Matt. 14:22-33
Healed woman of Canaan's daughter	Matt. 15:22-28
Healed a man who was deaf and dumb	Mark 17:31-37
Fed the 4,000	Matt. 15:32-39
Gave sight to blind man	Mark 8:22-26
Cured boy possessed of devil	Matt. 17:14-21
Coin in fish's mouth	Matt. 17:24-27
Restored sight to a man born blind	John 9:1-7
Healed crippled woman	Luke 13:11-17
Cured a man of dropsy	Luke 14:1-6
Raised Lazarus from the dead	John 11:43, 44
Cleansed ten lepers in Samaria	Luke 17:11-19
Gave sight to two blind men	Matt. 20:30-34
Healed ear of Malchus	Luke 22:50, 51
The miraculous draught of fishes	John 21:1-14

SOME OTHER BIBLICAL MIRACLES

OLD TESTAMENT

Aaron's rod becomes a serpent	Ex. 7:10-12
The ten Egyptian plagues	Ex. 7-12
Parting of the Red Sea	Ex. 14:21-31
Curing of the waters of Marah	Ex. 15:23-25
The manna	Ex. 16:14-35
Water from the rock, at Rephidim	Ex. 17:5-7
Death of Nadab and Abihu	Lev. 10:1, 2
Burning of the congregation at Taberah	Num. 11:1-3
Death of Korah, Dathan, and Abiram	Num. 16:28-33
Budding of Aaron's rod	Num. 17:8
Water from the rock, at Meribah	Num. 20:7-11
The brazen serpent	Num. 21:8, 9
Jordan's flow halted	Joshua 3:14-17
Fall of Jericho	Joshua 6:6-24
Staying of sun and moon	Joshua 10:12-14
Death of Uzzah	2 Sam. 6:7
Withering of Jeroboam's hand	1 Kings 13:1-6
The continuing oil and meal	1 Kings 17:10-16
Raising of the widow's son at Zarephath	1 Kings 17:17-24
Burning of the sacrifice on Mount Carmel	1 Kings 18:38
Dividing of Jordan	2 Kings 2:8, 14
Curing of the waters of Jericho	2 Kings 2:19-22
Supply of water to armies	2 Kings 3:9, 20
Multiplication of the widow's oil	2 Kings 4:1-7
Raising the Shunammite's son	2 Kings 4:32-35
Healing the poisonous food	2 Kings 4:38-41
Feeding 100 men with 20 loaves	2 Kings 4:42-44
Naaman's leprosy cured	2 Kings 5:10-14
An iron ax floats	2 Kings 6:5-7
Syrian army made blind	2 Kings 6:18-20
Dead man raised by contacting Elisha's bones	2 Kings 13:21
Destruction of Sennacherib's army	2 Kings 19:32-35
Sun reversed by ten degrees	2 Kings 20:9-11
Three Hebrews delivered from furnace	Dan. 3:19-27
Daniel delivered from lions	Dan. 6:16-23
Jonah, swallowed by fish, lives	Jonah 2:1-10

NEW TESTAMENT

Peter heals a lame man	Acts 3:1-11
Ananias and Sapphira struck dead	Acts 5:1-10
Paul converted on Damascus road	Acts 9:1-7
Peter heals palsied man	Acts 9:33, 34
Peter raises Dorcas to life	Acts 9:36-41
Angel delivers Peter from prison	Acts 12:5-17
Herod, supernaturally stricken, dies	Acts 12:23
Elymas, the sorcerer, smitten with blindness	Acts 13:6-11
Paul heals a cripple	Acts 14:8-10
Paul casts out a spirit of divination	Acts 16:16-18
Paul and Silas delivered from prison by an earthquake	Acts 16:25-27
Paul heals many at Corinth	Acts 19:11, 12
Paul restores Eutychus to life	Acts 20:9-12
Paul preserved from viper bite	Acts 28:3-6